# 10 FIRST STEPS FOR THE NEW CHRISTIAN

### by Woodrow Kroll

President
Back to the Bible

BACK TO THE BIBLE
LINCOLN, NE 68501

Copyright © 1992
by
The Good News Broadcasting Association, Inc.
All rights reserved.

143,000 printed to date—1996
(1160-220—10.5M—116)
ISBN 0-8474-0877-9

Unless otherwise noted, all Scripture quotations are from
*The New King James Version.*

Printed in the United States of America

# 10 First Steps for the New Christian

A prison keeper in the ancient Greek city of Philippi once asked two of his prisoners the most important question in life: "What must I do to be saved?"

The two prisoners, whose names were Paul and Silas, knew the answer: "Believe on the Lord Jesus Christ, and you will be saved" (Acts 16:31).

The prison keeper, who is sometimes called the Philippian jailer, did believe in Jesus; and he was saved. It is probable that he then turned to Paul and Silas and asked, "What shall I do now?" And they must have told him. For within a few hours he had taken several of the most important first steps that a new Christian should take.

Perhaps you, too, have just trusted Jesus Christ as your Savior. And perhaps you are asking, "What shall I do now?"

If so, this booklet is for you. Take these ten simple first steps for new believers, and your new journey to heaven will take on new excitement and purpose.

## Step one
# Make Sure You Are Saved.

There is only one requirement for salvation—faith in Jesus Christ. Just believe in Him. That's all you need to do.

You are not saved by belonging to a particular church or denomination; no church saves you! You are not saved if your good works outweigh your bad works; they never will!

You are saved *only* by faith in the Savior—Jesus Christ.

A man named Saul once struggled with the problem of how to please God. His story is found in the Bible.

Before he became a believer in Jesus, Saul had investigated all the possible "religious" things he might do to please God. He considered himself morally upright. Surely he had done enough "good" things to please Him.

But one day, while traveling on the road from Jerusalem to the Syrian capital of Damascus, Saul heard the voice of Jesus Christ. Suddenly he realized that he was a sinner, and by the power of God he was gloriously saved. His whole outlook on life was turned around. He would never be the same again, and later he became known as the apostle Paul.

After Paul believed in Jesus, he thought about how a person can be saved. He studied the Scriptures and reviewed his own personal experience, and he reached a conclusion: "A man is justified by faith apart from the deeds of the law"

4

(Romans 3:28). The great reformer Martin Luther came to the same conclusion. Millions of others have as well.

While Jesus was hanging on the cross, a thief hung beside Him on another cross. This thief turned to Jesus and said, "Lord, remember me when You come into Your kingdom" (Luke 23:42). No one could have spoken those words without real faith. He believed. Jesus responded, "Today you will be with Me in Paradise."

That thief had no opportunity to be baptized. There was no time to join a church, no chance to do good works. He was dying. All he had time to do was trust Christ.

Yet Jesus Christ turned to him and promised, "Today you will know the joy of full salvation."

There is only one requirement for salvation—faith in Jesus Christ.

But this faith must be yours alone. It must be personal. You are not saved because your parents believe. Your salvation doesn't come through someone else, not even your priest, your pastor or your rabbi.

Ephesians 2:8 says, "For by grace you have been saved through faith, and that not of yourselves; it is the gift of God." Notice the use of the personal pronouns—*you* and *yourselves*. Faith is personal.

---

*"More secure is no one ever,*
*Than the loved ones of the Savior."*
*—Lina Sandell*

---

Ralph Waldo Emerson said, "Souls are not saved in bundles." You must exercise faith in

Christ for yourself; and if you have, you are saved.

Once you have exercised faith, you are placed into the security of God's hand. Here is Jesus' promise to you: "My sheep hear My voice, and I know them, and they follow Me. And I give them eternal life, and they shall never perish; neither shall anyone snatch them out of My hand. My Father, who has given them to Me, is greater than all; and no one is able to snatch them out of My Father's hand" (John 10:27-29).

Have you trusted Christ as your Savior? If so, you are saved, secure in the hand of our Sovereign God. You couldn't be in a better position. You have taken the first step as a new Christian.

## Step Two
# Tell Someone.

After you have been saved, it's important to tell someone about it.

In the Bible we read about Andrew, a man who later became one of Jesus' disciples. When he trusted Jesus as Savior, he took an important first step. He told someone! In fact, he told his brother. John 1:41 says, "He first found his own brother Simon, and said to him, 'We have found the Messiah.'"

His explanation of his salvation was not very long, not very detailed and definitely not very theological. Andrew was a fisherman, not a theologian. Through the years he would learn more about God and become more theologically astute, but at this time he had just been saved. He simply told his brother what he had found.

No one expects you to have all the answers or all the right terminology just after you have been saved. God doesn't expect it of you. All you need to do is to tell someone what has happened to you. Tell that person that Jesus has become real to you, that He has come into your life and has saved you.

This doesn't make you a missionary, but it does make you a witness. Jesus wants us to be His witnesses (Acts 1:8).

Talking about your salvation may not be easy, and you may not comprehend everything that happened to you when you were saved.

But sharing your new life in Christ with others will help you in a number of ways. It will help clarify your thinking; you'll be able to separate the questions you have in your mind from the facts you know. It will also help solidify in your own mind what has happened to you. And it will bring your friends face to face with God's love for them.

> *"We have a story to tell to the nations, but it is also a story to tell to the neighbors."*
> *—Vance Havner*

One caution. When you tell someone what has happened to you, do not start an argument. People do not come to Christ at the end of an argument, but they frequently come to Him at the end of a testimony. Be genuine. Be kind. Be patient. Let the love of God that brought you to Him be reflected in the way in which you tell others about Him.

The greatest thing that will happen to you in your life is your salvation. Tell someone about it. Charles Wesley wrote:

> "O for a thousand tongues to sing
> My great Redeemer's praise,
> The glories of my God and King,
> The triumphs of His grace."

We don't have a thousand tongues, but we do have one. Let's use it for the noblest purpose possible—telling our friends, relatives and neighbors about what Christ Jesus has done for us. When you do, you have taken another first step for the new Christian.

The Son of God became a man so that men could become the sons of God. Tell someone.

## Step Three
# Establish a Quiet Time.

You need to grow in your new faith in Christ. And to do this, it is important for you to establish a quiet time.

By "quiet time" I do not mean a peaceful moment in a bubble bath. I mean getting alone with God and His Word.

In the hustle and bustle of modern life, we sometimes find it easy to live our lives with little or no regard for the God who saved us—or for His Word.

The Bible is the revelation of God's mind to you. It's what He wants you to know and do. Not only did God give His Son—the Living Word—to save you, He gave His Book—the Written Word—to guide you.

Many people own a Bible, but they never read it. For most people, it's an out-of-date book, good for their grandparents but not for them. Someone has said that if everyone blew the dust from their unused Bibles simultaneously, we'd all be killed in the dust storm.

To be sure, some sections of the Bible are difficult to understand, and some are not as exciting as others.

Once John Bunyan, the author of *Pilgrim's Progress*, said something like this: "I have sometimes seen more in a line of the Bible than I could understand; and yet at other times the whole Bible has been to me as dry as a stick."

Still, every section of God's Word has something to say to us, and that makes every passage very important.

> *"Never leave a passage of Scripture until it has said something to you."*
> —*Robert A. Cook*

When should you have your quiet time? It's important to read the Bible as often as possible. But I have found it helpful to have a specific time each day when I shut everyone out except God.

For me, that specific time is early in the morning. My mind is less cluttered then and my day is less complicated. Besides, God deserves me at my best, and the best part of my day is the first part. "O God, You are my God; early will I seek You" (Psalm 63:1).

Perhaps you will find another time of day suits your lifestyle better. That's fine. But make sure you establish a time and stick to it.

What should you do when you have your quiet time? Here is my six-step plan. It helps me make my moments with God and His Word more meaningful.

1. Start with prayer. Ask God to prepare you to meet with Him. If there is something in your life that you know displeases Him, confess it. Let Him forgive you so that nothing will hinder your communion together.

2. Read a specific portion of Scripture—perhaps a chapter or two. If you are not very familiar with the Bible, you may wish to start with the New Testament. Many people think that the Gospel of John is a good place to start. I also enjoy reading one or two of the Psalms every day.

3. After you have read a passage, meditate on it for a while. Think about what you read, and ask yourself what it means. What does God want

you to do? Remember, even though you may not understand all you read in the Bible, you can still obey what you *do* understand.

4. Write down questions about the passage as you read. I always keep a pen and paper nearby when I read my Bible. I write down the things I have learned from my reading and also the things I do not understand. Later I can find the answers to my questions from someone who knows about the subject, or I can find an explanation in a Bible commentary or some other Bible reference material.

5. Then read the passage again. Reading it the second time usually brings to light things you didn't notice the first time. This is a great way to learn on your own; for as you read, you'll have God's Holy Spirit as your teacher (John 14:26).

6. Finally, pray again. Thank God for sending His Son to die for you. Thank Him for giving you His Word—the Bible—because without it you would have no answers to life's big questions. Thank Him for teaching you from the passage you have just read.

One last thing. Many new Christians start a quiet time each day with great enthusiasm. But they soon get too busy. Their days fill up with activities, and other responsibilities press in upon them. And somehow God gets squeezed out.

Consistency is the key. The person who merely samples the Word of God never acquires much of a taste for it. You must come back to the banquet table of God's Word daily, just as you come to a table daily to eat physical food. Once you start, don't quit!

Come to your Bible regularly. Open it prayerfully, read it expectantly, trust it implicitly and live it constantly. It is true! The Bible that's falling apart usually belongs to someone who isn't. Take this third step for the new Christian—establish and keep a quiet time.

## Step Four
# Pray.

The best way to get to know a new friend is to spend time with him, to talk with him. And the best way to get to know God better is to spend time with Him, to talk to Him. That's what prayer is—simply talking to God.

You don't need to be afraid to approach Him. God welcomes your prayers and answers them. There are 667 prayers recorded in the Bible, and the answers to 454 are recorded. That is very encouraging.

The Bible is a book of prayer, and reading it and praying go hand in hand. This is illustrated by my suggestion that you begin and end your daily quiet time in prayer.

When should you talk to God? Actually, there is no wrong time. You can pray whenever you want to. But having a specific time to pray is as important as having a specific time to read His Word. When you pray, you talk to God. When you read His Word, He talks with you.

*"Prayer should be the key of the day and the lock of the night."*
*—Thomas Fuller*

Psalm 55:17 says, "Evening and morning and at noon I will pray." That's a good pattern, but not a magical formula. Actually, you need to pray more than that, and you dare not pray less.

The morning is an excellent time to worship God in prayer, to tell Him what He means to you and how much you love Him. It is a good time to praise Him for who He is and what He has done. It is a good time to seek guidance and blessing on all your activities of the day.

Noontime provides an opportunity for you to take stock of your day. Ask God if what you have done in the morning is pleasing to Him. If so, thank Him and ask for a similar afternoon. If not, confess your shortcomings of that morning and ask God to pave your path with His wisdom the rest of the day.

Evening can be a delightful time of thanksgiving and communion with God. Thank Him for your day, for your salvation, for His promises to you. This prayer time may not be as long as the morning time, because you may become tired and sleepy.

> *"No one in his senses, if he has any power of ordering his own day, would reserve his chief prayers for bedtime—obviously the worst possible hour for any action which needs concentration."*
> *—C. S. Lewis*

*How should you talk to God?* Perhaps you don't really know how to pray and you are wondering what you should say.

That's easy. Say what you would say to any good friend who loves you. You don't need a special vocabulary, nor do you need to be eloquent.

Don't be concerned if initially your prayers are short. Martin Luther once said, "The fewer words the better prayer." Luther wasn't suggesting that all prayers should be short. He was saying that a sincere prayer that uses only a few words is better than an insincere prayer that uses many.

Do not be concerned if you are not a polished "pray-er." God prefers sincerity to polish. If you cannot pray as you want, pray as you can. God knows your heart; He knows what you mean.

*Who can help you learn to pray?* If you are experiencing difficulty in learning to pray, here's some good news. When you pray, you are not on your own—Jesus, God's Son, and the Holy Spirit will help you in your prayer life. That's God's promise!

When you have sinned and need to talk to God about it, God's Advocate—His Son, Jesus—is there to help you. "And if anyone sins, we have an Advocate with the Father, Jesus Christ the righteous" (1 John 2:1). And when you don't know what to say, God's Intercessor—His Holy Spirit—helps you. "Likewise the Spirit also helps in our weaknesses. For we do not know what we should pray for as we ought, but the Spirit Himself makes intercession for us" (Romans 8:26).

*What should you pray for?* When men and women pray, they seldom ask for a change in character, but frequently they ask for a change in circumstances. That is a huge mistake. God controls our circumstances to improve our character. So do not get into the habit of pleading for a change in your financial or your physical condition when you pray. Allow your prayers to be a vehicle for God to shape your character into the character He intends you to become.

Prayer is the preface to purpose, the prologue to power and the prelude to peace. As soon as you have come to Christ as Savior, learn to come to the Father through Him in prayer. It's like talking with an old friend.

Don't let a day go by without talking to Him. He cares for you deeply and He wants you to get to know Him better. Spend time with Him daily.

## Step Five
# Make Christian Friends.

Someone has said that the ornaments of a house are the friends who frequent it. After you become a Christian, you may find a need for some new friends.

Don't totally abandon your old friends. You'll want to witness to them about your new faith in Christ.

But when you become a new creation in Christ Jesus—when old things pass away and all things become new—you may experience a sudden coolness on the part of your old friends, and many of them will likely abandon you.

Make sure you choose your new friends carefully. And be sure that they are not like your old friends who may have turned away.

Proverbs 4:14-15 tells us: "Do not enter the path of the wicked, and do not walk in the way of evil. Avoid it, do not travel on it; turn away from it and pass on."

> *"On the choice of friends our good or evil depends."*
> *—John Gay*

Your new friends will establish a setting in which you will build your new life. Make sure it is a righteous setting.

Choose friends who will help you through the ups and downs of your new Christian life.

This kind of friend will joyfully sing with you when you are on the mountain top and silently walk beside you through the darkest valley.

Aristotle said that a friend is a single soul dwelling in two bodies.

But Christian friendship goes deeper than that. Two *Christian* friends have the added advantage of the same Spirit residing in each of them—the Holy Spirit. "And by this we know that He abides in us, by the Spirit whom He has given us" (1 John 3:24). Paul mentions the "fellowship of the Spirit" (Philippians 2:1). He also mentions that we are of one Spirit, the Holy Spirit.

Your new friends can be a blessing and encouragement to you. Their friendship doubles your joy and divides your grief.

They can be a support for you; they can share their spiritual wisdom with you. The next best thing to being wise yourself is having a circle of friends who are wise. Ask them to help you understand what you need to know.

They can also help you in many other ways. They can help you find answers to your questions. They can help you in your Bible study. They can assist you in locating a church where you can worship and grow in the Lord.

Making Christian friends is an important step for a new Christian. But what if you don't know any Christians? Take the next step!

## Step Six
# Find a Church.

Soon after you trust Christ as Savior, you'll want to become part of a dynamic church. Not only will this help you make Christian friends, but it will help you grow by leaps and bounds in your new faith.

Church attendance has been declining over the past decades, especially in Europe and the Western World. Most people identify themselves with a particular church, but they never seem to be able to get out of bed to attend. You've heard about old Ed. He's a regular churchgoer; he never misses an Easter service. And that's the kind of attitude toward church attendance many people have today.

Why is it so important to become a part of a good church? There are many reasons. One is to worship God, to honor Him and His Word. The Bible cautions us not to fail to assemble together with other believers (Hebrews 10:25). The church in the first century, according to the Book of Acts, met together constantly. They praised God, they worshiped Him, and they learned about Him together.

A church exists for the double purpose of gathering in and sending out.

When we gather together in the church, we are blessed. But we don't go for a blessing. We go because we have a sense of calling, a sense of duty, a sense of need—a need for God and for others who have trusted Christ.

While we are in the church, our spiritual batteries are recharged so that we can be sent into the world to let our lights shine before men.

Someone will say, "I don't go to church because there are too many hypocrites there." If the church were perfect, you and I couldn't get in. The church is not going to be like heaven, but then nothing on earth ever will be.

But the true believers make up Christ's church (Matthew 16:18). He is the head of the church (Colossians 1:18). The church is His body (Ephesians 1:22-23). And when we attend a local church, we know that the people there are not perfect; but they are forgiven, and that's important.

What kind of church should you attend?

Here's a simple rule. Look for a church where the Bible is treated as God's Word—His authoritative Word—where people express a loving concern for those who are still lost in their sins and where the people worship God with deep respect.

> *"The church is not a gallery for the exhibition of eminent Christians, but a school for the education of imperfect ones."*
> *—Henry Ward Beecher*

I would avoid a church where you do not need a Bible during the whole service, where you never hear the name of Jesus Christ elevated and where no concern for lost sinners is ever expressed. In that kind of a church you must be careful. You may be in a mausoleum!

After coming to Christ as Savior, as soon as you can, find a good, Bible-believing church and become active in it. Do not delay. It's easy to lose interest in the church if you have never made an investment in it. Finding a church is an important step for the new Christian.

# Be Baptized.

There are some fine people who believe that baptism is necessary for salvation; but I disagree. Baptism is necessary for obedience, but not for salvation. True, Peter did say, "Repent, and let every one of you be baptized in the name of Jesus Christ for the remission of sins" (Acts 2:38). But the context of this verse does not link baptism with personal salvation, and neither should we. Besides, again and again *faith* is stated as the requirement for salvation, with no mention of baptism (John 3:16-18; 5:24; Acts 16:31; Romans 10:9-14).

If baptism does not wash away sins, what good is it? Why is it one of the ten first steps for a new Christian? Here are three reasons:

First, water baptism identifies our desire to obey Christ (Matthew 28:19-20). If you know that Christ wants you to be baptized and you refuse, you are being disobedient to your Master, the One who died for you.

Second, water baptism identifies our desire to be joined to Christ (Romans 6:1-4). We have no way to show to others how we are placed into the body of Christ when we are saved, except through the symbolism of water baptism. Being baptized shows that when Christ died, we died. When He was buried, we were buried. And when He rose from the dead, we rose from the dead—to walk in newness of life.

Third, water baptism indicates our desire to follow Christ (Romans 6:4). It symbolizes our final break with our old life, with the past and its sin. And although we will sin even after we are saved, being baptized tells the world we are headed in a new direction, we are on a new road, and we are taking the first steps on that road.

> *"We may never be martyrs but we can die to self, to sin, to the world, to our plans and ambitions. That is the significance of baptism; we died with Christ and rose to a new life."*
> *—Vance Havner*

Look at it this way. Following the Lord in baptism means doing what He did (Matthew 3:16-17). Following the Lord in baptism means telling the world you're under new management (1 Corinthians 6:19-20). Following the Lord in baptism means following Jesus and forsaking the way you used to live before you were saved (2 Corinthians 5:17). It is a way of telling everyone, "I'm a new person, a new creation in Christ. Old things have passed away; all things in my life have become new. I'm off to a brand-new start."

Baptism is going public for God. It is saying to the world, "I have decided to follow Jesus, no turning back, no turning back."

*Step Eight*
# Learn to Give.

Learning to give is one of the first lessons God teaches new believers. There is good reason for it too! Giving is important to God. In fact, one-sixth of the Books of Matthew, Mark and Luke and 12 of Jesus' 38 parables have to do with money.

There are three reasons why God places so much emphasis on our learning to give.

First, learning to give is important because of a divine pattern. God wants us to be like Him. He said, "Sanctify yourselves therefore, and be holy, for I am the Lord your God" (Leviticus 20:7; 1 Peter 1:13-16). And since God is a giver by nature, He wants us to learn to be givers as well. "For God so loved the world that He gave His only begotten Son" (John 3:16). Giving glorifies God because it makes us more like God.

Second, learning to give is important because giving is a biblical principle. Throughout the Bible we read about the principles of giving.

Giving is to be systematic (1 Corinthians 16:1-2); it is to be proportionate to your ability to give (1 Corinthians 16:2); it is to be sacrificial (Mark 12:43-44); it is to be spontaneous (Acts 2:45)—and more. Early in our Christian lives we should learn the biblical principles about giving.

Third, learning to give is important because of thankful praise.

Heart and hand go together. When your heart is filled with praise to God, your hand will express that praise by giving. Who is more deserving of your thanks than God? He loved you; He sent His Son to die for you; He saved you. Now you are taking steps to be conformed to the image of His dear Son, Jesus. And one of those steps is learning to give. After all, isn't "giving" the last half of the word "thanksgiving"?

> *"There are three kinds of giving: grudge giving, duty giving and thanksgiving. Grudge giving says, 'I hate to'; duty giving says, 'I ought to'; thanks giving says, 'I want to.'"*
> **—Robert Rodenmayer**

God loves a giver—one who has learned to give thankfully and cheerfully (2 Corinthians 9:7).

Each week set aside some of your time for God. You may do that through your quiet time or through service to Him in your local church. And each week set aside some of your income for God. You may then give it to your church and other ministries that have blessed you.

But whatever you do, get into the habit of giving back to God a portion of what He has generously given to you. Giving will make you a happy Christian, and it is one of the important first steps for the new Christian.

## Step Nine
# Memorize God's Word.

Memorizing God's Word is a privilege, not a duty. The benefit is all ours, but the pleasure is all His.

Memorizing Scripture takes both time and effort, so you need a good reason to do it. Here are three good reasons.

First, memorizing God's Word honors Him. Read Psalm 119 and notice the honor the writer heaps on God and His Word.

Verse 89: "Forever, O LORD, Your word is settled in heaven."

Verse 105: "Your word is a lamp to my feet and a light to my path."

Verse 140: "Your word is very pure; therefore, Your servant loves it."

Verse 162: "I rejoice at Your word as one who finds great treasure."

The reason the writer values God's Word so much is that he values God. God's Word is a reflection of Himself. It is a revelation of His mind. Memorizing Scripture is sometimes called hiding God's Word in your heart. When you do that, you are also hiding God there. Remember, God wrote only one book, and you honor Him when you show respect to that Book—the Bible—by hiding it in your heart. "Oh, how I love Your law! It is my meditation all the day" (Psalm 119:97).

A second good reason for hiding God's Word is to keep you from sin. The psalmist said it this way: "Your word have I hidden in my heart, that I might not sin against You" (Psalm 119:11).

When you are tempted to sin, you need a premier defense. God has provided that defense in His Word. If you have memorized portions of God's Word, you will be ready for Satan, the Tempter. When he badgers you and tries to get you to fall into sin, you will need your arsenal of Scripture.

There is a perfect example of this defense in the Bible. Early in His ministry, the Lord Jesus was severely tempted by Satan.

The first temptation took place in a barren wilderness. Jesus had been led to this place by the Holy Spirit and there He had fasted for 40 days. Satan knew He would be hungry, so he tempted Him with food. Jesus quoted Scripture (Matthew 4:4).

Then Satan took Jesus to the pinnacle of the temple, high above the Kidron Valley. There Satan tempted Jesus to throw Himself down off the pinnacle. Again Jesus quoted Scripture (Matthew 4:7).

Finally, the Tempter took the Lord to a high mountain and tempted Him with raw power, telling Him that all the kingdoms of the world would be His if He simply fell at Satan's feet in worship. Again Jesus quoted Scripture (Matthew 4:10).

Jesus is a tremendous example of what to do when you are tempted. If you have prepared yourself for temptation by hiding God's Word in your heart—by memorizing it—the Holy Spirit will bring those verses to your mind when you need them most. Remember, Bible verses will save you from spiritual reverses. Hide God's Word in your heart so you do not sin against Him.

A third reason to memorize Scripture is to prepare yourself to answer those who challenge your faith in Christ. In case you haven't noticed yet, not everyone is happy that you have become a Christian. Some of your old friends will do and say anything to get you to abandon your new faith. Your new life convicts them of the sin in their own lives. And when they come to you with silly questions, when they make fun of your faith, when they challenge your trust in the Savior, you will be glad you have memorized God's Word.

The apostle Peter counseled us with sage advice in 1 Peter 3:15. He said, "But sanctify the Lord God in your hearts, and always be ready to give a defense to everyone who asks you a reason for the hope that is in you, with meekness and fear." Since you never know when you will have to give that defense, you must be ready always. This requires memorizing Scripture consistently. It is one of the important first steps for a new Christian.

## Step 10
# Find an Accountability Friend.

You increase your ability, stability and responsibility when you increase your sense of accountability to God. One way you can do this is to find another believer who will be your accountability friend.

What is an accountability friend? It is a mature Christian who agrees to disciple you, to help you grow and mature in your new faith in Christ. It is someone who agrees to hold you accountable, someone who will help you carry through on what you determine to do.

If you tell your accountability friend that you are going to have a quiet time every morning for half an hour, he or she will call you later in the day and ask if you did. An accountability friend makes sure that you do all that you told God you would do.

But the accountability street goes both ways. Frequently two people will be accountability friends for each other. They will hold each other up and lift each other up when they need a lift. And if one should fall, the other will help him or her up.

There is a striking image of this in Ecclesiastes 4:9-10: "Two are better than one . . . For if they fall, one will lift up his companion. But woe to him who is alone when he falls, for he has no one to help him up."

This principle works not only when you take a physical tumble but also when you have a weakness in the spiritual realm. If you have an accountability friend, you know that someone is there for you when you stumble, someone who will help you to keep from falling. For example, if you lose your enthusiasm in your walk with the Lord and become lukewarm, your accountability friend can take you aside and kindly, sincerely warn you that you are in spiritual danger.

An ancient proverb from the Near East says, "A friend is one who warns you." But an accountability friend, a true friend, never stops with a warning. He will also pray with you, encourage you and guide you back on the right track. That's what accountability friends are for.

---

*"My best friend is the one who brings out the best in me."*
*—Henry Ford*

---

Friends don't just criticize, they help. A true friend doesn't sympathize with your weakness; he helps you summon your strength. When you and another Christian make a commitment to be accountable to each other, the best will be brought out in both of you.

# A FINAL WORD

Have you recently come to Christ as your Savior? If so, it is important for you to start your Christian life right. Now that you have new life you need to grow, for growth is as important as birth. What a tragedy it would be if a tiny baby were to remain small all of his life. But it would be equally tragic if you were born again but never grew spiritually.

These ten steps for the new Christian do not constitute a magical formula. But they are derived from God's Word and have been successfully practiced by mature Christians for generations.

If you take these first steps on the road to heaven, you'll find the journey to be a challenge and a blessing. But more than that, your first steps will not be your last. God bless you as you step out for Him.

# Acknowledgments

**Page 13**

Quotation by C.S. Lewis
From *Letters to Malcolm: Chiefly on Prayer*
Copyright by Harcourt Brace Jovanovich, Inc.
Used by permission.

**Page 23**

Quotation by Robert N. Rodenmayer
From *Thanks Be to God*, By Robert N. Rodenmayer
Copyright Harper and Row, Publishers, Inc.
Used by permission.

Back to the Bible is a nonprofit ministry
dedicated to Bible teaching, evangelism and
edification of Christians worldwide.

If we may assist you in knowing more
about Christ and the Christian life, please
write to us without obligation.

**Back to the Bible**
P.O. Box 82808
Lincoln, NE 68501